Magazine: The Cut-Up Asemics

Scott
Helmes

Post-Asemic Press

Post-Asemic Press 010

ISBN: 978-1-7328788-8-4

post-asemicpress.com

Contact: postasemicpress@gmail.com

Postasemicpress.blogspot.com

Cover art by Scott Helmes and Michael Jacobson

THE MANY STYLES OF SCOTT HELMES
Dr. John M. Bennett

Scott Helmes' early move from textual poetry into decades of dynamic activity as a visual and asemic poet has resulted in some truly unique and spectacular work that he has published internationally in experimental and visual poetry journals, and in books and chapbooks (often in exquisite limited editions). He has also done large scale works and prints presented in art galleries, at times as murals or wall and other installations that transform the spaces they occupy. Whether all this work can be considered poetry or art (it is both, at the same time) is irrelevant to the quality and impact of it, but it is notable that he has called many of his pieces "haiku" or "sonnets", in that they observe some of those forms in terms of shape and/or lineation, but do so without using a single "word".

This book in black and white and gray-scale (Helmes also works extensively in color) brings together many of the techniques he has mastered: torn bits of text and image, cut-up text and letters, drawing, collage, painting, and rubber stamping. His techniques of smearing rubber stamps across paper, using them as ink brushes, really, has been widely adopted, rarely as successfully, by other visual poets, including myself. *Magazine: The Cut-Up Asemics* also shows the wide range of styles he has mastered: from the clean, sharp structures derived from typographic elements, to collage, to expressionistic gestural ink drawings, and every possible combination of these processes. Helmes is a trained professional architect, and his strong sense of design is one of the great strengths of his work, but it is a sense of design liberated and informed by an expressionistic freedom that at times takes one's breath away. His works may be "asemic" in a technical sense, but they are far from meaningless: they communicate the thinking and emotionality of a unique and strong artistic literary mind and personality, and reward endless contemplation. This book is a treasure.

August 2019

2706 ～～～～ BONES I

Flowers XLIII   2 IV 06

Bones XI   7 II 06

Bones VIII   25^II 06

BONES XXXIII m 22 VII 60

Bones XV 16ᵗʰ Dec

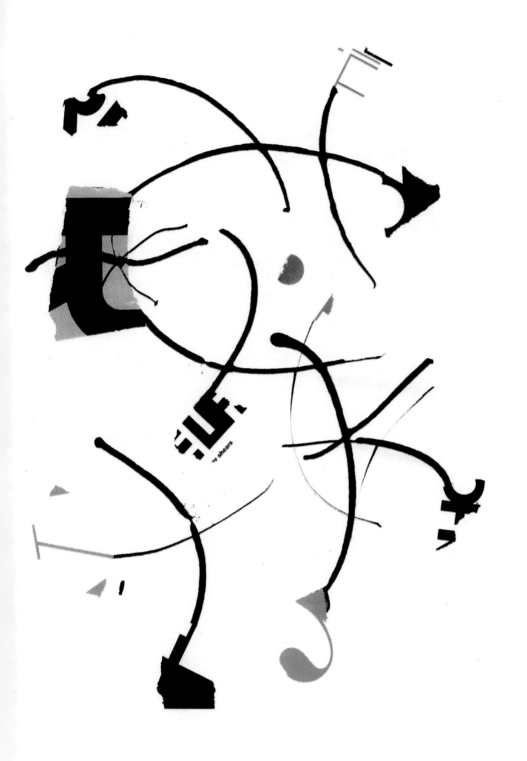

Bones XXIX 28 VIII/10 [signature]

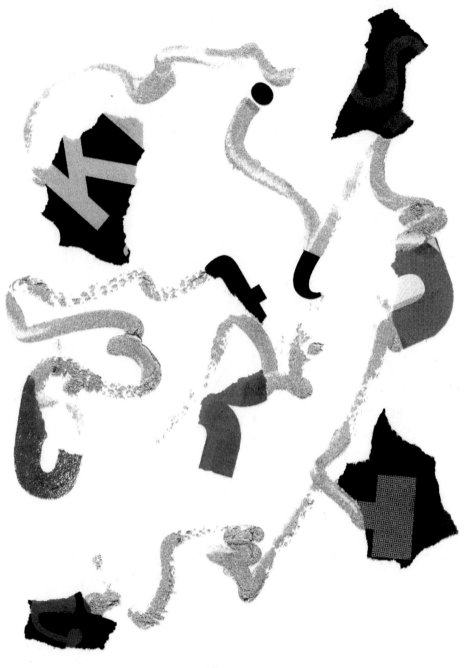

12 FX 11

Bones XXXIV   25 VII 10

Icones XXXII   14^{IV}/_{10}

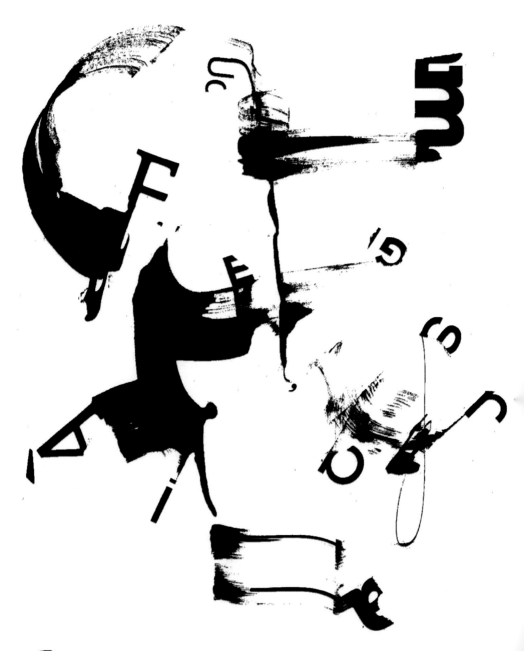

28ⅩⅡ13

14 ^F/15

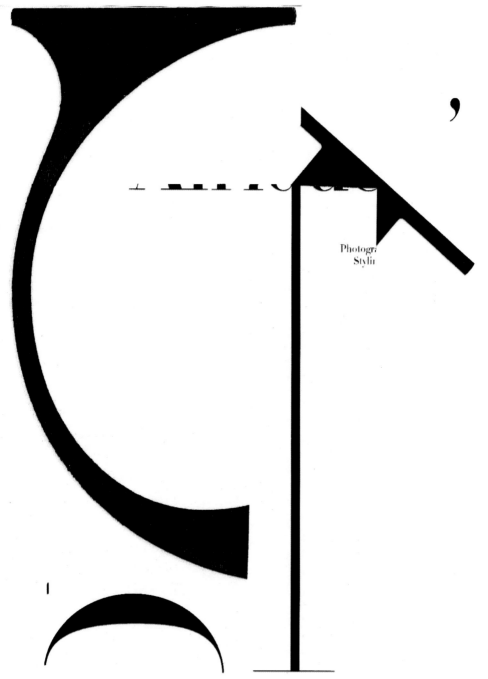

Photogr
Styli

24 III 1.

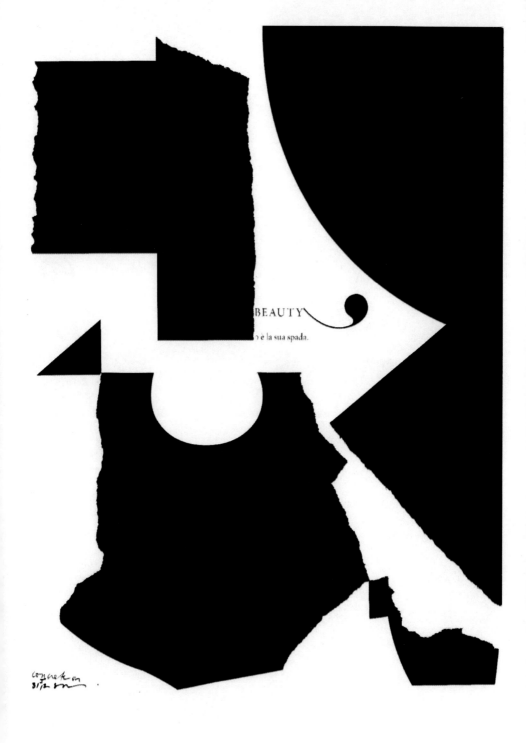

BEAUTY

è la sua spada.

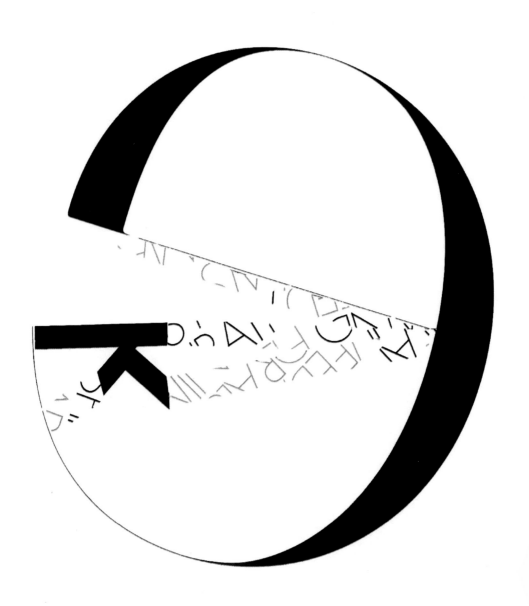

8 IX/8

concrete on 19 VIII 12   SM

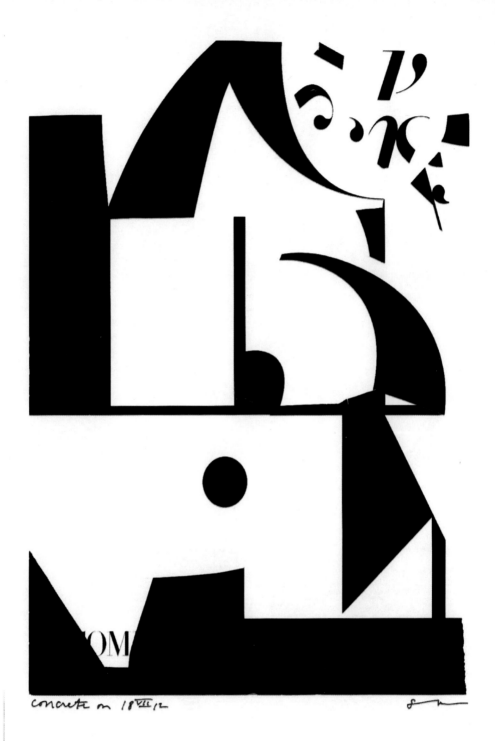

concrete m 18 $\overline{VII}$ 12

30ᴵ13

15⁻75   S~~~~

Bran XXXV   9/72 10   [signature]

Bones XVIII 8/8/07

3⊤/8

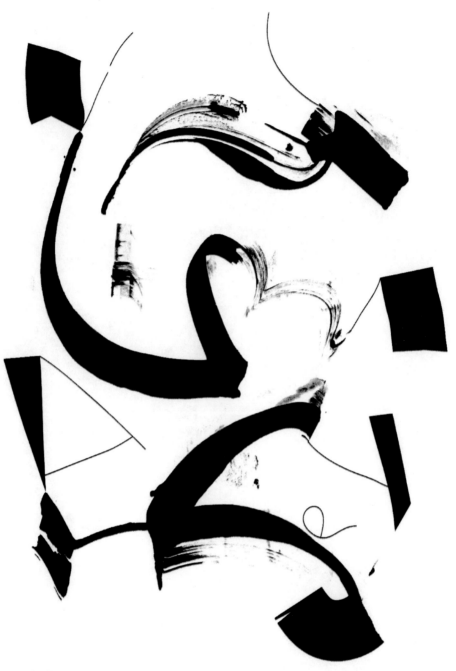

29.7.13

6 IX 78

18 XII/12   Sm

15⁴⁴⁄₇₂

28I13

12 VIII 12

6 IX 78

27/10   Sm

30 06 BONES X

Bones VIIIA   6ᵗʰ06 Sᵍ~

BONES IX

BONES II

22-XI-17

re the no

BONES II   21/96 ⟨signature⟩

Bones Akin   20 Dec   JM

Bonum IV   [signature]

Bones XI   19 III 06

23/7   Sm

Scott Helmes is a poet, book artist, writer, artist, architect and photographer. His experimental poetry has been collected, published and exhibited worldwide for over 40 years. Books include *1000 Haiku*, Stamp Pad Press; *Poems From Then to Now*, Redfoxpress (Ireland), and *The Last Vispo Anthology: Visual Poetry 1998-2008*, Fantagraphics. In 2015, two works were included in *The New Concrete*, an international concrete poetry anthology from Hayward Press, London. 13 poems were published as part of the Kobitadihi Online Magazine *World-wide Visual Poetry*, April 2017. An altered book was exhibited in the *Wallpaper* exhibition at Traffic Zone in July, 2018. His studio is located in Minneapolis, MN, USA.

Made in the USA
Monee, IL
17 August 2020